EVEREST

THE REMARKABLE STORY OF
EDMUND HILLARY AND
TENZING NORGAY

ALEXANDRA STEWART

ILLUSTRATED BY
JOE TODD-STANTON

BLOOMSBURY
CHILDREN'S BOOKS
NEW YORK LONDON OXFORD NEW DELHI SYDNEY

For my parents, Christopher and Donna Stephens —A. S.

BLOOMSBURY CHILDREN'S BOOKS
Bloomsbury Publishing Inc., part of Bloomsbury Publishing Plc
1385 Broadway, New York, NY 10018

BLOOMSBURY, BLOOMSBURY CHILDREN'S BOOKS, and the Diana logo
are trademarks of Bloomsbury Publishing Plc

First published in Great Britain in May 2019 by Bloomsbury Publishing Plc
Published in the United States of America in February 2020
by Bloomsbury Children's Books

Bloomsbury books may be purchased for business or promotional use. For information on bulk
purchases please contact Macmillan Corporate and Premium Sales Department at
specialmarkets@macmillan.com

Library of Congress Cataloging-in-Publication Data
available upon request
ISBN 978-1-5476-0159-2 (hardcover)
ISBN 978-1-5476-0160-8 (e-book) • ISBN 978-1-5476-0161-5 (e-PDF)

Art created digitally
Book design by Claire Jones
Typeset in English Engravers Roman and Zemke Hand ITC
Printed in Italy by Elcograf S.p.A., Verona
10 9 8 7 6 5 4 3 2 1

All papers used by Bloomsbury Publishing Plc are natural, recyclable products
made from wood grown in well-managed forests. The manufacturing processes
conform to the environmental regulations of the country of origin.

To find out more about our authors and books visit www.bloomsbury.com and sign up for our newsletters.

BIBLIOGRAPHY

Coburn, Broughton, *Triumph on Everest: A Photobiography of Sir Edmund Hillary* (2003)

Douglas, Ed, *Tenzing: Hero of Everest* (2003)

Hillary, Sir Edmund, *View from the Summit* (1999)

Hunt, John, *The Ascent of Everest* (2013)

Norgay, Tenzing and James Ramsey Ullman, *Man of Everest: The Autobiography of
    Tenzing* (1956)

AUTHOR ACKNOWLEDGMENTS

My profound thanks to: Saskia Gwinn from Bloomsbury for giving me the
opportunity to write this book, Camilla Knight for her inspiration, and
Ed Douglas and Jake Meyer for their expert advice. My heartfelt
appreciation also goes to Elaine Connolly and Claire Jones from
Bloomsbury for their hard work and patience; Joe Todd-Stanton
for bringing words to life with his stunning illustrations;
and Chris Haley, Jen Turpin, and Tom Hillary for
their help. Above all, I am indebted to my husband,
Jonty, and our children, Flora and Jake,
for their love, support, and good humor.

TABLE OF CONTENTS

⤖ INTRODUCTION ⤕

At 11:39 in the morning on May 29, 1953, a beekeeper and a former yak herder took a final few weary steps onto a snowy dome.

Exhausted and breathing hard, they could go no further—there was nowhere further to go. It was then that Edmund Hillary and Tenzing Norgay realized they had done it. They had climbed onto the roof of the world. Satisfied—and perhaps a little surprised—the pair gazed down on the earth below from a height at which no person had stood before.

The sun shone in the piercing blue sky and a gentle breeze was blowing. This incredible success had come after months of painstaking preparation, years of training, and a lifetime of ambition and dreaming. Along the way they had battled perilous physical conditions, illness, and intense fear.

This book tells their story—the story of two unlikely heroes from humble backgrounds whose grit, determination, and modesty captured the hearts and imaginations of the world, two ordinary men who battled against the odds to be the first to achieve an extraordinary feat. But as brave, resourceful, and determined as they were, this success did not belong just to Hillary and Tenzing.

This was a hard-won victory built on the experience, knowledge, and efforts of hundreds of people from around the world.

This is their story too.

Hillary and Tenzing prepare for their
greatest challenge: conquering Everest.

WHY CLIMB EVEREST?

"Because it's there." —George Mallory, 1923

What made Hillary and Tenzing's achievement all the more remarkable was that they had triumphed where so many others had failed before. Climbers had been trying to reach the top of Everest for more than thirty years.

A huge amount of time, effort, and money—not to mention national pride—had been invested in these attempts. Despite this, each one had ended in disappointment, and some even in death.

Part of the Himalaya mountain range, Everest sits on the border of Tibet and Nepal.

Everest was first measured by the British Survey of India in the 1850s and identified as the tallest mountain in the world—standing at 29,002 feet above sea level.

More recent measurements put Everest at 29,029 feet high. However, debates about its exact height still rumble on.

What we can say is that Everest is roughly equal in height to twenty Empire State Buildings piled on top of one another. Or, to put it another way, just lower than the cruising height of a jumbo jet.

Colonel Sir George Everest

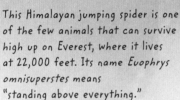

This Himalayan jumping spider is one of the few animals that can survive high up on Everest, where it lives at 22,000 feet. Its name *Euophrys omnisuperstes* means "standing above everything."

After they had made their initial measurement, the British named the mountain in honor of a former British Surveyor General of India—a Welshman named Colonel Sir George Everest.

Locally, however, it already was known by several different names. To the Nepalese, it is *Sagarmatha*, meaning "Goddess of the Sky."

In Tibet, it is known as *Chomolungma*, which to some means "Goddess Mother of the World." To Tenzing, however, it meant "The Mountain So High No Bird Can Fly Over It."

Everest is an extreme place. At the highest points on the mountain, conditions are so harsh that no animal or plant can survive.

Temperatures can plunge to -76°F and powerful winds of more than 100 mph buffet the summit for most of the year. Meanwhile, violent storms can dump up to 10 feet of snow at a time.

Bar-headed geese

For a few weeks each year the weather conditions improve just enough for climbers to make an attempt on the summit. Yet, even during these "weather windows," conditions remain hazardous.

Low oxygen levels and the draining effects of high altitude on the human body mean that climbers must battle for every step they take.

The path to the top is lined with danger, including avalanches, tumbling towers of ice, rockfalls, and seemingly bottomless crevasses.

Back in the early 20th century, however, one major difficulty of climbing Everest lay in gaining access to it.

His Holiness the 13th Dalai Lama of Tibet

At first, neither the Tibetans nor the Nepalese would allow foreigners to travel to the area. It was only in 1921 that His Holiness the 13th Dalai Lama granted a British team of climbers and surveyors permission to visit it. Their aim was to discover if a route to the summit existed. The race to climb Everest had begun . . .

~ PART ONE ~

THE STORY OF TWO VERY DIFFERENT CHILDHOODS

Edmund Percival Hillary
Family Tree

PERCIVAL
} AUGUSTUS { — — } GERTRUDE {
HILLARY   CLARK

JUNE   EDMUND   REXFORD
} HILLARY { — — } PERCIVAL { — — } FLEMING {
CARLILE   HILLARY   HILLARY

Edmund Percival Hillary was born on July 20, 1919, in Auckland, a city on New Zealand's North Island.

"**Ed**," as he would become known, was the second of three children. He had an older sister named June and a younger brother named Rex.

Their father, Percy, had fought in the First World War in the infamous Gallipoli Campaign. In 1916, after being shot through the nose and catching dysentery, he was sent back home to New Zealand. Not long afterward, he married Ed's mother, a schoolteacher named Gertrude Clark.

Percy set up a newspaper in a small town called Tuakau. But he was also very interested in beekeeping. Over time, he established hundreds of hives producing gallons upon gallons of honey, which he would then sell. Eventually, he would earn enough money to resign from the newspaper and became a full-time beekeeper.

Growing up in Tuakau

The hills and fields of Tuakau provided an ideal playground for young Ed, who was something of a dreamer. Inspired by the adventure stories he loved to read, he would disappear for long walks, carrying a stick that he would pretend was a sword.

However, Ed's childhood was far from perfect. Despite being able to conjure up a good bedtime story, his father was a strict man who held staunch beliefs about how things should be done. Ed and his father often clashed, which resulted in Ed developing a strong and spirited character.

Ed's childhood home surrounded by beehives

Going to school

Ed encountered his first real challenges at school. As a young boy, he would walk barefoot the half-mile to Tuakau Primary School, whatever the weather. His mother's patient coaching meant that he progressed well at school, and he was able to skip a couple of years. However, this was not necessarily a good thing for Ed, who found himself by far the youngest in his class. He struggled to make friends and was a shy and quiet pupil.

When he was just 11, his parents sent him to Auckland Grammar School. Here, his classmates were a full two years older, and he was terrified. Once again, he found himself alone and friendless. When lunchtime arrived, he would escape to the back of the school, where he would sit and watch a colony of ants busy at work. These ants—he would later say—were the only friends he really had during that bleak time.

Nevertheless, things eventually began to improve for Ed. He performed well in class and began to grow taller and stronger. By his final year of grammar school, he had begun to enjoy himself.

ED STARTS CLIMBING

It was at this time that Ed persuaded his father to let him join a school trip to New Zealand's Mount Ruapehu.

Here Ed saw snow for the very first time, spending ten carefree days skiing and climbing around the mountainside. This was the moment that sparked Ed's lifelong passion for snow and mountains.

But just as Ed was settling into his stride, he left school and enrolled at a university in Auckland, where the family had recently moved. He was just 16 years old, but his mother was ambitious for him and insisted he should go. He chose to study math and science, subjects he had performed well in at school.

During the holidays, Ed helped out with his father's beekeeping business. He and Rex would work seven days a week, lugging huge boxes and cans of honey around the farm, which now boasted 1,600 hives. The work was tough and entirely unpaid. On the upside, however, it helped transform Ed into a physically and mentally strong young man.

Unfortunately, his success at school would not continue. Two years into his university career, having passed no exams and made no friends, Ed decided it was time to leave.

Ed helps out his father, a small-town beekeeper, during the summer.

Meanwhile, far away from New Zealand, the clouds of war were gathering. When Great Britain declared war on Nazi Germany in 1939, New Zealand mobilized their armed forces, too. Ed now had a vital chance to spread his wings. Always ready for adventure, he immediately applied to join the Royal New Zealand Air Force. However, he was frustrated to learn that he would have to wait a while before he could begin training.

Climbing Mount Ollivier

In an attempt to console himself, Ed headed off for a short break in New Zealand's Southern Alps. One evening, he saw two fit and tanned young men returning to the hotel in which he was staying. They had just climbed Mount Cook, New Zealand's highest mountain, standing at 12,219 feet. Ed marveled at their achievement and longed for similar adventure in his own life. So the next day, he hired a guide and climbed a far smaller mountain nearby, named Mount Ollivier. When he eventually reached the top, he gazed upward to the summit of Mount Cook and promised himself that one day he would climb it too.

Little did he imagine that this resolve would eventually help him scale the world's highest mountain.

Ed scales Mount Ollivier and dreams of conquering even higher mountains.

11

WAR

At the beginning of 1944, Ed was called up for training in the Royal New Zealand Air Force. His training camp was based in New Zealand's Wairau Valley.

Never one to waste an opportunity, Ed used his weekends to climb the surrounding mountains. One in particular was larger than the rest. This, of course, was the one that Ed most wanted to tackle.

One winter weekend, he set out alone to climb the 9,465-foot peak. Despite the treacherous weather conditions, which locals believed would see him perish on the mountainside, he succeeded.

Unconcerned by his brush with danger, Ed was simply delighted that at last he had climbed a "decent" mountain.

After completing training as a navigator on Catalina flying boats, Ed was posted to the Solomon Islands for search and rescue duties. Off duty, Ed spent time exploring the coastal waters in an old motorboat.

One day, while returning from a short trip, the boat's gas tank caught fire. Ed was badly burned and forced to abandon the blazing boat and swim ashore.

He was taken to a US naval hospital for life-saving treatment. Nearly half his skin had been burned off and he was lucky to be alive.

Despite the seriousness of his injuries, Ed recovered quickly.

BACK HOME

By now, the war was drawing to a close and Ed was determined to get back to New Zealand.

Eventually, Ed was allowed to fly back to Auckland. He arrived home with two goals: to return to beekeeping and to do as much climbing as he could.

Ed stayed true to his ambitions. He spent the next few years working in his father's honey business and using every moment of his spare time for mountaineering. A chance meeting with the famous New Zealand mountain guide Harry Ayres proved a pivotal moment for Ed. Under Harry's expert eye, Ed grew in skill and confidence.

Ed travels to the Himalayas

Ed became a talented and assured climber. So, when his great friend and fellow climber George Lowe suggested he join him on a trip to the Himalayas with a group of other experienced New Zealand mountaineers, Ed jumped at the chance.

The expedition left New Zealand in May 1951. They traveled by plane, ship, train, and finally by foot to the Himalayas. There they climbed a number of towering, snowy summits that had not been scaled before.

Climbing in the Himalayas was a remarkable new chapter in Ed's climbing career. But while Ed was a newcomer to the mighty peaks of the Himalayas, the man who would share his success on Everest already knew and loved them intimately.

Ed climbs his way toward his greatest achievement.

Tenzing Norgay
Family Tree

GHANG LA MINGMA — **DOKMO KINZOM**

KIPA · **KESANG** · **TENZING NORGAY** · **THAKCHEY** · **CHINGDU**

SONAM DOMA

Tenzing Norgay was born in 1914 in Tibet's Kharta Valley, a remote area close to Everest.

It is believed Tenzing was born by a sacred lake called Tshechu. According to the local Tibetan holy men, the place and time of his birth made him a lucky baby. These holy men, known as lamas, told Tenzing's parents that if they looked after their baby well, he would grow up to be great. Tenzing's childhood was difficult. Living conditions were harsh, and eight of his parents' fourteen children died before they reached adulthood. Sadly, their names were not recorded.

Growing up with yaks

Tenzing's father, Mingma, was a yak herder. His job was to look after a large group of yaks that belonged to a local monastery. Work was a family affair. In the summer, the family took the yaks higher up the mountain slopes to graze on the rich grass, and in the winter, they would move farther down the mountainside to where they owned a house.

The animals lived in the bottom of the house while the adults and children lived on the floor above. The smell of the animals, the smoke from cooking, and the general hubbub would etch themselves on Tenzing's memory. Despite the hardships, Tenzing and his family were happy.

Tenzing's family share their house with yaks in the winter.

Tenzing's Everest ambition

When he was old enough, Tenzing began working too. There was always plenty to be done, from growing potatoes, barley, and corn to tending the sheep and, of course, the yaks. What Tenzing enjoyed most of all was wandering with the yaks along the mountainsides. Far above him, towering over the tops of all the nearby mountains, was the mighty Everest.

The mountain fascinated the young Tenzing. Despite the many warnings from lamas of the gods, goddesses, demons, and terrible creatures that stalked its snowy peaks, Tenzing longed to explore it. As a young boy, he had seen Western expeditions coming up the Kharta Valley and he knew that, while some people had died trying to climb Everest, most had not. He later wrote, "What I wanted was to see for myself, find out for myself. This was the dream I have had as long as I can remember."

Tenzing gazes at Everest; his dream is to climb to its summit.

MOVE TO KHUMBU

While Tenzing was still a young boy, his family moved to the Khumbu region of Nepal.

Khumbu is the home of many Sherpa people, whose mountaineering expertise is prized by explorers in the Himalayas. The success of Sherpa men, who worked as expedition porters and guides during the long and dangerous mountain climbs, made Tenzing determined to follow in their footsteps.

However, it was not just the mountains that caught Tenzing's imagination. While the other boys played, he would sit by himself and daydream about adventures in far-off lands. When his parents packed him off to a monastery with the hope that he would eventually become a Buddhist monk, he ran straight back home.

At 13, he ran away again—this time from home to Kathmandu, the capital of Nepal. Finding himself more than a little homesick, he returned after a couple of weeks.

Nevertheless, the desire to escape and explore the wider world beyond his home remained strong.

Tenzing considers making the
long journey to Darjeeling.

Tenzing and his wife, Dawa Phuti

TREK TO DARJEELING

In 1932, when he was 18 years old, Tenzing made his move.

Taking just a blanket with him, Tenzing joined a group of young men and women who were trekking from Khumbu to Darjeeling. Darjeeling is an Indian town in an area of the Himalayan foothills made famous by the excellent tea it produces. At that time, Darjeeling was also the jumping-off point for expeditions to the Himalayas. Here, at the old Tea Planters' Club, mountaineers would recruit Sherpas to work as their guides and porters. It was the perfect place for the adventurous Tenzing to seek his fortune.

The trek was hard going and took several weeks. When Tenzing eventually arrived in Darjeeling, the only work he could find was as a cowhand. Nobody wanted to hire him as a porter on their expedition because he had no experience—but how could he get any experience if nobody would hire him? It was not until 1935, three years after his arrival in Darjeeling, that Tenzing received his first chance.

This was also the year he married Dawa Phuti, a Sherpani (Sherpa woman) who had also traveled from Khumbu to Darjeeling. Desperate to provide a better life for his new wife, Tenzing once again sought employment on an expedition to Everest.

TENZING STARTS TO CLIMB EVEREST

The expedition was led by a famous British explorer named Eric Shipton.

Although Shipton had already hired a team of Sherpas, he made a last-minute decision to add two more to the team. Around twenty men lined up with Tenzing in the hope of being chosen. Shipton later wrote that he chose Tenzing, despite his lack of experience, "largely because of his attractive grin." It was a unique and infectious grin that would, almost twenty years later, become famous throughout the world.

Although the expedition did not get very high up the mountain, Tenzing worked hard and performed well. He was among the Sherpas who carried loads up to the North Col (the first camp established when mountaineers climb Everest from the Tibetan side), at more than 23,030 feet, before bad weather forced them to retreat. It was here, on the Col, that Tenzing realized he was different from the other Sherpas on the expedition. While they were happy to head back down the mountain, Tenzing wanted to climb higher.

More trips to Everest

After the expedition, Tenzing returned to Darjeeling, where Dawa Phuti gave birth to their first child, a son named Nima Dorje. However, Tenzing did not stay around for long. The next three years saw him play a key role in a number of expeditions—including two more to Everest.

The first, in 1936, was thwarted by the early arrival of the monsoon (a season of heavy snowfall that makes climbing Everest next to impossible). The second, in 1938, was more successful for Tenzing. Although attempts to reach the top were halted by deep snow, Tenzing himself excelled.

A line of Sherpas hoped to join Shipton's expedition.

He carried heavy loads to a height of more than 27,000 feet—higher than he had ever been before. His efforts won him recognition as a strong and valuable team member as well as a Tiger Badge—a highly prized award given only to the most outstanding Sherpas.

The world begins to change

Within the space of three years, Tenzing had transformed his life. Once a penniless cowhand, he was now respected and sought-after as a professional Sherpa.

Meanwhile, in the winter of 1938, his wife gave birth to their second child, a girl named Pem Pem. But, just as things were beginning to look up for Tenzing, events conspired against him. As the world went to war in 1939, large-scale expeditions to the mountains ceased. Tenzing instead found work with the Indian Army as an assistant in an officers' mess. Then, later that year, tragedy struck. His beloved son, Nima Dorje, died. The boy was just four years old.

Not long afterwards, Dawa Phuti gave birth to the couple's third child, a girl named Nima. Five years later, disaster struck again when Dawa Phuti took ill and also died. A heartbroken Tenzing was left with two young daughters to care for.

He quickly married again. His new wife, Ang Lhamu, was warm, clever, and kind, and when Tenzing struggled to find work immediately after the war, she supported the family by working as a nanny.

Tenzing's bright smile made him stand out from the crowd.

ANG DAWA

EARL DENMAN

BACK TO EVEREST

The tough times continued until 1947, when Tenzing received his first opportunity to go back to Everest.

However, this was not a usual expedition. It was the idea of a Canadian adventurer called Earl Denman. Denman had climbed some mountains in Africa and thought he was experienced enough to try his luck on Everest. He arrived in India with very little money, limited equipment, and no permission from the Tibetans to climb the mountain. He asked Tenzing to go with him to act as a porter and a guide.

Although he knew the trip was bound to fail, the pull of Everest was too strong for Tenzing. He agreed to help Denman and persuaded his friend and fellow Sherpa Ang Dawa to join him. As Tenzing had expected, the attempt was a total failure. The trio did not get very far up the mountain before the cold and their lack of equipment and preparation defeated them.

GIUSEPPE TUCCI

TENZIN GYATSO

Tenzing becomes a sirdar

Undeterred, Tenzing returned to Darjeeling and immediately signed up for an expedition to climb some mountains in the Garhwal region of India with a group of Swiss climbers. It was on this expedition that he first took up the honored position of sirdar. A sirdar is the name given to the Sherpa who manages and organizes the other Sherpas and porters on an expedition.

In 1948, he travelled to Tibet with the eccentric Italian scholar and explorer Giuseppe Tucci—an expert in Tibetan and Nepalese history. It was during this trip that Tenzing first met the Dalai Lama Tenzin Gyatso, who was then just a 13-year-old boy.

Three years later, he was sirdar on a French expedition to India's second highest mountain, Nanda Devi, during which two French climbers, Roger Duplat and Gilbert Vignes, lost their lives.

More Himalayan expeditions followed. With each one, Tenzing became more experienced and more determined to climb higher—higher, indeed, than anyone had climbed before. But, having been put on ice for the duration of the war, the serious quest to climb Everest did not resume until 1951. And it would be 1952 before Tenzing returned to its slopes.

ROGER DUPLAT
&
GILBERT VIGNES

⤜ PART TWO ⤛

THE RACE FOR EVEREST

Before the 1950s, there were seven major expeditions in total to climb Everest. Alongside these were two foolhardy attempts that, without the backup of an experienced team, had no chance of succeeding.

1921: The first British Everest reconnaissance expedition to the mountain took place in 1921. Its aim was to find out if there was an achievable route up the mountain. George Mallory was one of two climbers to reach the North Col of Everest at an altitude of around 23,030 feet.

1922: The second British Everest expedition to the mountain was the first serious attempt to reach the top. George Mallory was, once again, among the party of climbers. The highest point reached by team members, using oxygen, was 27,300 feet. During this expedition, seven Sherpa climbers were killed in an avalanche below the North Col, the first reported deaths on Everest.

1924: In the third and most notorious British Everest expedition to the mountain, Edward Norton set a record of reaching 28,126 feet without oxygen. This height was not exceeded for 29 years, or for 54 years by a climber without oxygen. On the same expedition, George Mallory and his climbing partner, Andrew Irvine, disappeared while attempting the summit using oxygen. Their fate fueled the international obsession with Everest. Mallory's body was eventually found 75 years later.

1933: The fourth British expedition to Everest involved a new generation of climbers. The team included the renowned explorer Eric Shipton. Two attempts were made on the summit, without oxygen, both of which failed. The highest point reached on this expedition was 28,100 feet.

1934: This was the year an eccentric Yorkshireman named Maurice Wilson attempted to climb Everest alone. Poorly equipped and with no mountaineering experience, Wilson believed that his inner faith would see him to the top. Setting up camp at the base of the North Col, he asked his Sherpas to wait ten days for him to return, after which they would be free to leave. When he failed to come back, the Sherpas left for Darjeeling. Wilson's body was found a year later at the foot of the North Col.

1935: The fifth British expedition was a small one led by Eric Shipton. It was a reconnaissance expedition—paving the way for a more serious attempt the following year. This was Tenzing Norgay's first trip to the mountain as a young porter. Although the team reached the North Col with two weeks of supplies, bad weather and the threat of avalanches prevented them from going any farther up the mountain.

1936: The 1936 expedition was formed of a large, strong, and experienced group. It included Eric Shipton as well as Tenzing Norgay, who was returning for the second time as a porter. The team did not get far up the mountain before hopes of reaching the top were dashed by the early onset of the monsoon, which made climbing impossible.

1938: The seventh British Expedition took place in 1938. It was smaller and less expensive than previous expeditions. The team established a camp at 27,200 feet, but attempts to summit were halted by deep snow. This was Tenzing Norgay's third expedition to Everest.

1947: A Canadian-born electrical engineer named Earl Denman attempted to climb Everest from the north, along with Sherpas Ang Dawa and Tenzing Norgay. The trio reached the foot of the North Col. However, realizing he was hopelessly ill-equipped and unprepared for the huge challenge ahead, a cold, weak, and dejected Denman was forced to admit defeat and turn back.

Some of the brave climbers who joined expeditions to Everest.

AN INTERNATIONAL RACE

The aftermath of the Second World War saw great political change in the Himalayan region.

In 1950, the Chinese invaded Tibet and closed off its borders. This meant that the traditional route up Everest, from the north, was now out of bounds. But as one door shut, another opened.

A bloodless revolution in Nepal resulted in the once mysterious and isolated kingdom opening up to outsiders. Under the new regime, foreigners were granted one permit to climb Everest per year. This meant that other nations—not just the British—now had a shot at reaching the summit. The race to scale Everest had turned into an international affair.

Eager to claim what they believed should be their prize, the British were quick out of the starting blocks.

The British survey the southern path

In 1951, a British party received permission for the first reconnaissance of Everest from the south. The expedition was led by Eric Shipton, a veteran of four pre-war expeditions. Among the team was Edmund Hillary, fresh from his first Himalayan adventure. Ed had written to Eric offering his services. To his surprise, Shipton accepted.

Soaked by the monsoon rains and attacked by blood-sucking leeches, the men battled their way up and down deep valleys and dizzying ridges. Eventually the rain stopped and Ed saw Everest in its full majesty for the first time. He later described how his heart thumped in his chest with the excitement of the moment.

The first stage of Shipton's plan was to climb a nearby peak to get a better view of the lower slopes of Everest. He would then be able to see if a route up the mountain existed. He invited Ed to join him. As the pair looked down from their vantage point, they were amazed to discover that a route did indeed exist. It would be treacherous and tricky, but it might just work. Unfortunately, because this was just a fact-finding expedition, the team was not equipped to climb very far up Everest. However, they did have the time and expertise to tackle the first challenge of the route: the Khumbu Icefall . . .

Eric Shipton with his reconnaissance team.

THE KHUMBU ICEFALL

The Khumbu Icefall is one of the most infamous parts of Everest, claiming more lives than any other part of the mountain.

It is a half-mile wide river of ice that flows down the mountainside at a rate of around 3 feet per day.

Avalanches often come thundering down from the slopes above, burying anyone in their path.

The constant movement makes the area highly unstable and dangerous. It is pitted with terrifyingly deep crevasses. Some of these are made yet more lethal by a thin covering of snow that hides them from climbers.

Huge blocks of ice the size of houses can tumble down without warning. Meanwhile, steeple-sized towers of ice, called seracs, are at risk of sudden collapse.

It was through this maze of ice that Ed and his fellow climbers carefully picked their way. When they eventually reached the top, they found their way blocked by a huge crevasse.

They were forced to retreat. However, they left the mountain confident that they would return the following year with the equipment and know-how to try for the top. Little did they know that the rug had just been pulled from under their feet . . .

Tenzing and Lambert are defeated by the mighty Everest.

A SWISS ATTEMPT

Back in Kathmandu, the Nepalese had given a world-class team of Swiss climbers permission for two expeditions to Everest the next year.

This meant that Ed and the British team would have to wait until 1953 for their next shot. But by then it might be too late to be first to the top. All they could do was wait and see how far their rivals would get.

Their first attempt

Led by the outstanding climber Raymond Lambert, the Swiss had chosen Tenzing to be their sirdar. In 1952, an elated Tenzing gave his all to the climb—investing every last ounce of his strength and energy from start to finish. His dedication meant he was chosen to make an attempt on the summit, along with Lambert.

Together, they battled against the trials of bad weather and faulty oxygen gear to reach the highest point anyone had ever gotten to on Everest. But they faltered at 28,210 feet, just 84 feet higher than Edward Norton's 1924 record. Exhausted, starved of oxygen, and unable to go any further without facing certain death, they turned and headed back down the mountain.

A second try

A second attempt, in the autumn, was curtailed by the arrival of winter. To make matters worse, Tenzing's fellow Sherpa, Mingma Dorje, was killed by falling ice. His death was the first on Everest since that of Maurice Wilson, twenty years previously.

Two grueling expeditions had taken their toll on Tenzing's health. Weak, miserable, and on the verge of collapse, he was admitted to a hospital. As he lay recovering in bed, he received a letter from a Major Charles Wylie. The letter threw him into deeper turmoil; it was an invitation to join the British on their 1953 expedition to Everest as sirdar. Despite his weakened health, Tenzing knew he had to accept. "This time," he told a friend, "I will climb or die."

Tenzing receives a letter in his hospital bed.

PART THREE

HILLARY AND TENZING CLIMB EVEREST

The stakes were high as the British team began preparing for their expedition in the autumn of 1952.

In all likelihood, this would be the British team's final chance to claim victory on Everest. The French had won permission to try their luck in 1954, the Swiss were on track for another attempt the following year, and the Americans were also vying for a turn.

The team is assembled

It was vital to make this the best effort yet. So, because of their expertise and experience, it made sense to ask Hillary and Tenzing to join them. Under the leadership of Colonel John Hunt, a serving army officer and mountain warfare expert, a team of experts combed the world for the most advanced gear available, and every aspect of clothing and equipment was rigorously researched and tested.

The expedition was planned with the precision of a military campaign.

Ready to start the great expedition that lay ahead of them, the team members assembled at the British embassy in Kathmandu in March 1953. They were probably the best prepared expedition ever to have set out for Everest. It was here, on the ambassador's lawn, that the whole team met for the first time. This was also the first time that Hillary and Tenzing had ever met. Hillary later recalled being struck by Tenzing's flashing smile, writing that it was impossible not to be "warmed by his charming manner." Little did he know then that the names "Hillary and Tenzing" would become worldwide news.

Hillary and Tenzing meet for the first time at the British embassy in Kathmandu.

MARCHING TO EVEREST

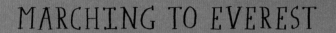

The team and their army of 350 porters set off on their march to Everest.

Over the next seventeen days, they carried more than eight tons of baggage (equivalent in weight to five cars) for over 150 miles, across ridges, valleys, and foaming rivers, to the foot of Everest.

During their journey, the climbers became fitter and their bodies gradually adapted to the higher altitude. This vital process is known as acclimatization.

On March 26, the expedition arrived at Tengboche Monastery—perched at 12,000 feet on a high ridge. Here, they began a training period during which they got to know their surroundings, their equipment, and, most importantly, each other.

Training complete, they moved off to start their mission—but not before receiving a blessing from the head lama for the success of their expedition. The team established their base camp at the foot of the Khumbu Icefall. It was from here that they would launch their attack.

The team carry their heavy equipment to Tengboche Monastery.

EVEREST SURVIVAL GUIDE

Humans need oxygen to survive. We get it by breathing the air around us, which contains oxygen mixed with other gases. The higher you go, the thinner the air becomes and the less oxygen there is to breathe. At the summit of Everest, three breaths provide about the same amount of oxygen as one breath at sea level, so you have to breathe much harder to get the oxygen your body needs.

ACCLIMATIZATION

To cope with the thinner air and lower oxygen levels at high altitude, our bodies must adapt. This process is known as acclimatization.

To give their bodies a chance to acclimatize, climbers should ascend slowly to high altitudes.

Climbers who don't acclimatize properly can suffer from something called Acute Mountain Sickness (AMS). Symptoms of AMS range from headaches, nausea, exhaustion, confusion, and dizziness to a life-threatening build-up of fluid in the lungs (pulmonary edema) or brain (cerebral edema).

Even those who do acclimatize will still feel the effects of high altitude. These can include breathlessness, a faster heart rate, coughing, loss of appetite, and trouble sleeping.

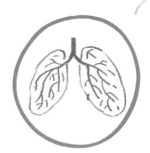

EXTRA OXYGEN

Today, most climbers use bottled oxygen to get to the summit of Everest. This helps them combat the effects of high altitude and improves their performance.

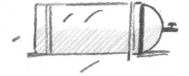

But, in the days of Mallory and Irvine, debates raged about whether using oxygen was necessary or "sporting." It was not until Hillary removed his breathing apparatus at the top of Everest that scientists knew for certain that humans could survive on the summit without extra oxygen—at least for a short time.

The Italian climber Reinhold Messner in 1978 became the first person to climb Everest without extra oxygen.

OTHER DANGERS

Frostbite: This is the freezing and ultimate death of body tissue. Frostbite generally occurs in bits of the body that are farthest from the heart, including the fingers, toes, nose, ears, cheeks, and chin. It can cause permanent numbness or loss of use of the affected area. In the worst cases, the body part must be amputated.

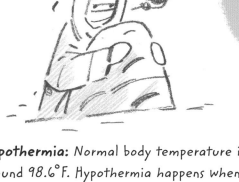

Hypothermia: Normal body temperature is around 98.6°F. Hypothermia happens when someone's body temperature drops below 95°F. At such a low temperature, the heart, nervous system, and other vital organs can't work properly. If untreated, hypothermia can lead to death. Hypothermia is usually caused by being in a cold environment for a long time.

Dehydration: Without enough water, the human body cannot work properly. Dehydration happens when more fluid is lost by the body than is replaced by drinking liquids. The risk of dehydration is greater for mountaineers because our bodies lose water more quickly at high altitude. The symptoms of severe dehydration include confusion and weakness. If left untreated, dehydration is fatal.

High altitude cough (Khumbu cough): Breathing cold air quickly and deeply can cause the lining of a climber's lungs to dry out and become inflamed. The resulting irritation causes the climber to cough—often quite violently. People have been known to break ribs as a result of the Khumbu cough.

PLAN IN ACTION

Hunt's plan was to make two attempts on the summit, each by a pair of climbers.

Hunt would decide the names of these four key individuals at a later date. But first, the whole team and their supporting Sherpas needed to focus on shifting supplies up the mountain.

Starting from Base Camp, members of the climbing team would forge a path upward. Along the way they would establish eight more camps. Meanwhile, the Sherpas would follow, carrying supplies from camp to camp. Their ultimate aim was to ensure that the highest of these camps would be equipped with the food, oxygen, fuel, and other key gear required for the final push to the top.

This would be a slow and laborious process, with climbers and Sherpas carrying loads of up to 40 pounds (about the weight of a 3-year-old child), moving up and down the mountain multiple times. Along the way they contended with treacherous snow and ice conditions, appalling weather, stomach troubles, sore throats, and hacking coughs, not to mention the weakening effects of high altitude.

So, although just a select few would get a shot at the top, they would only get that chance thanks to everybody's efforts.

Hillary leads the team through the Khumbu Icefall

The first major obstacle the climbers had to overcome was the Khumbu Icefall—tackled successfully by Hillary in 1951.

Hillary was delighted when he was chosen to take the lead in establishing a route through this hazardous and ever-shifting labyrinth of ice. Hoping to be chosen to try for the summit, he and a small team attacked the challenge with gusto.

Their efforts were sabotaged by heavy snow and tumbling ice, which obliterated their tracks. Nevertheless, they eventually forced their way through to the top—before turning their hand to making the route more safe and stable for the Sherpas who would follow. This required cutting steps into the ice with their axes, fixing lines of rope for the Sherpas to hold on to, slinging rope ladders down vertical ice walls, and using aluminum roofing ladders to bridge deep crevasses.

When the ladders ran out, the team used tree trunks brought up from the nearest forest—which was a three-day hike away.

Hillary and Tenzing team up

At one stage, Hillary very nearly lost his life while trying to leap across a crevasse. As he landed on the far side, the ice broke off beneath him and he plunged downward. But Tenzing, who was attached to Hillary by a rope, saved the day. With lightning speed, Tenzing immediately thrust his ice ax into the snow and wrapped the rope around it. The rope pulled tight, stopping Hillary's fall. Impressed by his skill, Hillary realized that he and Tenzing had the makings of a strong summit team. From then on, he used every opportunity to demonstrate this to Hunt.

But there were further dangerous obstacles to overcome before they could even think about the summit . . .

The climbers trek through the hazardous route on Everest.

THE JOURNEY UP

The expedition team faced new challenges and different dangers as they continued their death-defying ascent of Everest.

The Western Cwm

After the Khumbu Icefall, the climbers worked their way up a gently rising valley called the Western Cwm (pronounced "koom," a Welsh word for steep-sided valley). Here, the sun's strong rays reflecting off the snowy slopes could cause temperatures to rocket to 98°F, exposing the climbers to severe sunburn and dehydration. But, when the sun set, the thermometer would plunge below freezing once more.

SUMMIT
29,029 FEET

SOUT
SUMM
28,700

NORTHEAST RIDGE

CAMP
27,900 fe

SOUT
FAC

THE SOUTH COL, 25,800 feet: Nineteen Sherpas reached the South Col, helping to carry over 700 pounds of vital gear (tents, oxygen, food, fuel, cookers, climbing equipment). The final staging post for the first of the two summit attempts.

BASE CAMP: At the foot of the Khumbu Icefall, it was surrounded by pinnacles of ice.

BAS
CAM
17,900

The Lhotse Face

At the head of the Western Cwm lay their next great challenge, a treacherously steep ice slope known as the Lhotse Face. To ensure the supplies could be carried up the 4,000-foot slope safely, a special party of climbers and Sherpas spent time cutting steps and fixing ropes up it. The work was thwarted by illness, heavy snow, and extreme cold. But above all, lack of oxygen eroded the men's ability to move and even think properly. One of the team, George Lowe, later said, "I thought I was going extremely well; in fact, I was staggering about like a man in a dream." With the monsoon season closing in, Hunt was worried that slow progress on the Lhotse Face would terminate the expedition. But somehow the team forced a way up. "It was a performance," Hunt later said, "that should go down in mountaineering history."

Camp 9: Hillary and Tenzing spent their final night on this narrow ledge before summiting.

NUPTSE
25,680 FEET

EAST
GE

LHOTSE
27,890 FEET

SOUTH
COL

DEATH ZONE

CAMP 8
25,800 feet

LHOTSE FACE

CAMP 7: The halfway point on the punishing climb between Camp 5 and the South Col.

CAMP 7
24,000 feet

CAMP 6
23,000 feet

WESTERN CWM

CAMP 5
22,000 feet

ADVANCE BASE CAMP: Up to 30 men lived in a village of tents while providing support to the climbers.

CAMP 4
21,200 feet

KHUMBU
GLACIER

The top of the Khumbu Icefall

CAMP 3
20,200 feet

MP 2
00 feet

CAMP 2: A rest point for those ferrying equipment up the mountain. The team later abandoned this camp because the violent ice movements made it too dangerous.

KHUMBU ICEFALL

KHUMBU ICEFALL: Sherpas carried over three tons of stores through this hazardous maze of moving ice. The trail needed to be in the middle of the icefall to avoid avalanches.

The South Col

Next came the South Col—a freezing, desolate moonscape of rock and ice, continually swept by fierce winds so powerful that to Tenzing they sounded like "the roar of a thousand tigers." At 26,000 feet, the climbers had now entered the Death Zone. At such a height, the concentration of oxygen in the atmosphere is so low that nothing can live for any length of time—not even with supplementary oxygen. It was from here that a smaller team would now attempt the summit. And that team would have to make their move quickly.

TOM BOURDILLON AND CHARLES EVANS ATTEMPT THE SUMMIT

Hunt had decided that the first pair to try for the top would be two of the team's strongest and most experienced climbers: Tom Bourdillon and Charles Evans.

Bourdillon and Evans would do this using a new type of oxygen gear called the closed-circuit system. Designed by Bourdillon and his father, this breathing apparatus was more efficient than the traditional system because it did not require the user to carry heavy spare cylinders of oxygen. This would enable Bourdillon and Evans to climb directly from the South Col—without having to spend a night at a higher camp.

The pair started out promisingly on May 26, reaching the South Summit—the second highest peak on Everest at 28,700 feet—by 1:00 p.m. But just over 300 feet short of the top, they reached a crisis point. Their breathing equipment had been acting up from the start. Short of energy, oxygen, and time, they were forced to turn around.

Continuing would have placed them in mortal danger and jeopardized the entire expedition. They returned dismayed. All hopes were now pinned on Hunt's second summit team: Hillary and Tenzing.

Bourdillon and Evans turn back as they run out of oxygen and energy.

HILLARY AND TENZING TRY FOR THE TOP

Using the tried and tested open-circuit oxygen equipment, Hillary and Tenzing set out from the South Col on May 28.

They were supported by George Lowe, Alf Gregory, and Sherpa Ang Nyima, who went ahead to establish a route upwards. This would help Hillary and Tenzing conserve their energy for the final push.

At 27,350 feet, they reached a store of supplies left for them by John Hunt and Sherpa Da Namgyal two days previously. Each of them piled extra gear on their backs—including oxygen cylinders and a tent. They were now carrying 50 pounds each, except for Hillary, who was carrying over 60 pounds—slightly heavier than a 7-year-old child or 27 bags of sugar.

At 27,900 feet, they found a narrow shelf on which to pitch their tent. Their support team took off their loads and, after wishing Hillary and Tenzing luck, set off back down the mountain to the South Col.

The team pitches a tent to rest before attempting the final climb.

After taking two hours to set up their tent, Hillary and Tenzing crawled inside. They filled themselves up on cookies, sardines, chicken noodle soup, and canned apricots, washed down with a hot lemon drink, before settling down for the night. As the wind picked up, Hillary worried that they might be blown off the edge of the mountain. But, after putting on their oxygen masks, they were able to snatch four hours of sleep.

Hillary and Tenzing rest the night before their greatest challenge.

When their oxygen quota ran out, they awoke feeling cold and wretched. With their supplies carefully calculated, they could not afford to waste any more time on such luxuries as sleep.

At 4:00 a.m. on May 29, Hillary and Tenzing began to prepare for their final departure. Hillary had removed his boots before going to sleep and, with the temperature at –16°F, they had frozen solid. He had to thaw them out over the Primus stove before he could pull them on again.

At 6:30 a.m. the pair set off toward the South Summit.

As the slope became steeper, the conditions grew worse. With the deep and unstable snow shifting under their feet, both Hillary and Tenzing knew there was a strong chance they would be swept off the mountain. Gripped by fear, they decided to keep moving forward to the South Summit, where they were relieved to find conditions improved.

From the South Summit, they continued on to the summit ridge. Moving steadily but cautiously, they came to a vertical rock face that was 40 feet high. This was the final obstacle standing between them and the top.

Wondering how on earth they could climb up it, Hillary noticed that a thick layer of ice clinging to the face of the rock had begun to break away. Taking a chance, he squeezed into the crack between the rock and the ice and, with every ounce of his strength, wriggled his way up to the top. Tenzing quickly followed. Had the ice given way under their weight, they would have plunged down the mountain to certain death.

Once at the top, the pair wasted no time in continuing their journey upward. Moving slowly and sapped of energy, they began to wonder how much longer they could go on for. But before these thoughts could take hold, they found themselves standing on a patch of snow surrounded by nothing but sky in all directions . . .

Hillary makes a daring vertical climb, supported by Tenzing.

THE VIEW FROM THE TOP

Below them were the other mighty Himalayan peaks of Makalu and Kangchenjunga, and to the north stretched the Tibetan plateau.

They had done it. As Hillary moved to shake Tenzing's hand, a euphoric Tenzing threw his arms around Hillary.

It was a historic moment, but with their limited oxygen supplies, the pair had little time to revel in their triumph! Hillary removed his oxygen mask and quickly pulled out his camera. He photographed Tenzing standing on the summit with his ice ax raised and the United Nations, Indian, Nepalese, and Union Jack flags, which were tied to it, fluttering in the wind.

He then photographed the views down the mountain, to provide evidence that they had indeed reached the top. Meanwhile, Tenzing dug a hole in the snow and placed hard candy, chocolate, and a colored pencil given to him by his daughter inside it. These were offerings to the spirits of Everest, giving thanks for their safe passage.

Hillary performed a similar ritual, burying a crucifix that John Hunt had asked him to leave at the summit. Finally, the pair removed the flags from Tenzing's ice ax and pushed them into the snow. Their time up, they turned around to retrace their steps down the mountain.

Hillary did not think to ask Tenzing to take a photograph of him. After all, he later said, the summit of Everest was no place to teach a novice how to use a camera.

Exhausted but satisfied, Hillary and Tenzing start their descent.

Meanwhile, at Advance Base Camp on the Western Cwm, John Hunt was waiting nervously for news. It was not until the following afternoon that he discovered what had happened . . .

George Lowe had waited for Hillary and Tenzing on the South Col and they trekked back to the camp together. As they approached the team, Hillary and Tenzing were too tired to shout or wave but an ecstatic Lowe waved his ax at the summit. Hunt rushed to greet them and, with tears in his eyes, threw his arms around Hillary and Tenzing.

EVEREST CONQUERED!

Hillary and Tenzing triumph!

NATIONAL HEROES

It was not long before the whole world knew of the expedition's success.

James Morris, *The Times* correspondent who had accompanied the expedition, rushed to an army radio post in the nearby town of Namche Bazaar, where he sent a coded message to the British embassy in Kathmandu.

This was deciphered by the ambassador and sent on to London, arriving on the eve of Queen Elizabeth II's coronation. The next day, news of the expedition's success was splashed across the front pages, with journalists hailing it the "crowning glory."

Back in Nepal, Hillary and Tenzing had little idea what a stir their climb had caused. It was not until they started walking back to Kathmandu that they began to get an inkling. They began to receive daily mailbags containing letters, telegrams, and newspaper clippings celebrating their success. One mailbag contained a message for Hillary announcing that the Queen had made him a knight of the British Empire!

Astounded by the news, Hillary's first thought was that he should buy a new pair of overalls. After all, a knight could not be seen in scruffy clothes—even if he was a beekeeper.

EDMUND HILLARY

(Mountaineer)

TENZING NORGAY

(Sirdar)

COLONEL JOHN HUNT

(Expedition leader and army officer)

DA NAMGYAL

(Sherpa)

ANNULLU

(Sherpa)

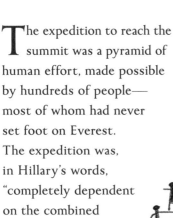

ANG NYIMA

(Sherpa)

Some of the 38 Sherpas who were part of the expedition team. Nineteen Sherpas reached the South Col, six of them twice!

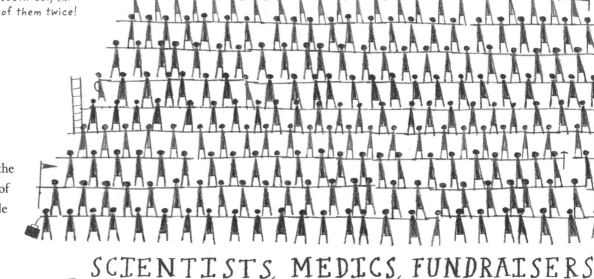

SCIENTISTS, MEDICS, FUNDRAISERS, MANUFACTURERS, DIPLOMATS, FAMILIES

The expedition to reach the summit was a pyramid of human effort, made possible by hundreds of people—most of whom had never set foot on Everest. The expedition was, in Hillary's words, "completely dependent on the combined effort of all those lower down."

HUMAN EFFORT

R. CHARLES EVANS

(Surgeon)

GEORGE BAND

(Cambridge student)

TOM BOURDILLON

(Rocket scientist)

ALF GREGORY

(Travel agent)

GEORGE LOWE

(Teacher)

WILFRED NOYCE

(Schoolmaster)

DR. MICHAEL WARD

(Doctor)

MIKE WESTMACOTT

(Oxford student)

MAJOR CHARLES WYLIE

(Gurkha officer)

DR. GRIFFITH PUGH

(Physiologist)

TOM STOBART

(Cameraman)

JAMES (JAN) MORRIS

(*The Times* correspondent)

RAYMOND LAMBERT

(Swiss expedition leader)

GRIFFITH PUGH set out two important food rations: one to be eaten lower down the mountain and one higher up. Climbers had to melt snow to drink water!

RAYMOND LAMBERT nearly made it to the top with Tenzing in 1952. The British team was able to learn from the information he generously shared with them.

EQUIPMENT

1. Warm hats were needed, but for parts of the climb Hillary wore a handknit cotton sun hat, made by his sister.

2. Tents and other equipment were tested in a wind tunnel in Farnborough, UK, to ensure they would stand up to Everest's extreme weather.

3. Special lightweight boots with heavy steel crampons were important for gripping ice and snow.

4. Hillary's ice ax was made of steel with an ash-wood handle.

5. The expedition crew wore clothes made from the finest Shetland wool.

6. The team wore long string underwear beneath several layers to keep them warm and dry.

7. Sleeping bags made in Canada, New Zealand, and the UK were three times as heavy as modern sleeping bags. Higher up the mountain, sleeping bags were laid out in patterns as signals to those below.

8. Aluminum ladders for bridging crevasses were made in Wales.

9. High-energy food such as sugar, milk powder, cookies, candy, oatmeal, cheese, tea, lemonade powder, and soup were all important. Hillary chose sardines and canned apricots for his attempt on the summit.

10. Rope was made from hemp.

11. Walkie-talkies made of rubber and produced in Cambridge, UK, were essential for communication with the lower camps. The batteries needed to be kept warm next to their skin. Today, people can use mobile phones on Everest!

12. Consisting of three oxygen cylinders, the breathing apparatus weighed 40 pounds (like carrying a five-year-old child).

~ PART FOUR ~
THEIR STORIES CONTINUE AFTER EVEREST

The weeks and months following the expedition were a whirlwind for Hillary and Tenzing.

After Nepal, Hillary, Tenzing, and the rest of the team traveled to India to meet Prime Minister Nehru. From there they flew to Britain, where they received a rapturous welcome.

Parties and receptions were held in their honor, and bags of fan mail rolled in. Some letters to Hillary even contained offers of marriage.

During a garden party at Buckingham Palace, the Queen officially knighted Hillary by touching him on both shoulders with a sword. From then on, he would be known as Sir Edmund Hillary, affectionately known as Sir Ed.

Tenzing, meanwhile, received the George Medal—the highest civilian award for bravery in Britain.

The Queen knights Hillary for his great achievement.

Ed goes home

Edmund Hillary eventually returned home to New Zealand, where more excitement awaited him. On September 3, 1953, after a short engagement, Ed married his girlfriend Louise. The grinning newlyweds emerged from church under an arch of ice axes to begin their life together.

After the initial frenzy surrounding his success had died down, Ed returned to beekeeping. At the end of 1954, Louise gave birth to their son, Peter, and in 1955 their daughter Sarah was born. But while Ed was happy living a peaceful family life, the lure of adventure proved too much to resist, and it wasn't long before he was off again.

Ed and Louise marry in Auckland, New Zealand.

A troop of vehicles treks across Antarctica.

CROSSING ANTARCTICA

Since childhood, Edmund Hillary had been fascinated by the adventures of the polar explorer Ernest Shackleton.

In 1914, Shackleton had led a doomed expedition to cross the continent of Antarctica from sea to sea, via the South Pole.

In 1956, the British Commonwealth Trans-Antarctic Expedition set out to succeed where Shackleton had not. This time, however, they would use modern equipment to help them.

Their plan was to drive tracked vehicles across 2,000 miles of ice and snow, from the Weddell Sea coast to McMurdo Sound, via the South Pole. The vehicles to be used included modified farm tractors. However, the team would also employ the more traditional dogs and sleds to help them along the way.

When the expedition leader, Dr. Vivian "Bunny" Fuchs, asked Ed to head up his support team, Ed accepted the challenge. Ed and a group of New Zealanders were tasked with establishing a base on the opposite side of Antarctica from Bunny's team. From here, he and his men would drive toward the South Pole, laying food and fuel dumps along the way. These "depots" would ensure Bunny and his team could complete their crossing.

The expedition moves south

The team's journey south was torturously slow and nail-bitingly dangerous. As well as blizzards and extreme cold, they faced the constant threat of plunging down cavernous crevasses. For safety, they roped their vehicles together and traveled in one line. On more than one occasion, the driver of the lead tractor found himself dangling into an abyss before being hauled out by the vehicles behind.

The men traveled at a top speed of 3 mph. Despite this, they still managed to outpace Bunny's team. Although it had not been part of the original plan for him to go all the way to the South Pole, a confident Ed decided to make a dash for it and wait for Bunny there. On January 4, 1958, after more than 80 days, the New Zealand team completed their 1,250-mile journey to become the first people ever to drive to the South Pole.

Bunny and his team arrived at the South Pole sixteen days later, before going on to complete their historic crossing of Antarctica on March 2, 1958.

The treacherous route was plotted carefully.

YETI HUNT

After so much time away from his family, Ed was relieved to return to New Zealand.

Safely back at home, he resumed his beekeeping and was delighted when Louise gave birth to their third child, a daughter named Belinda.

But offers of further travel and exploration kept rolling in and, in 1960, Ed set off on another expedition. This time it was back to the Himalayas with his old Everest teammate Dr. Griffith Pugh. The pair had received sponsorship from an American publishing firm to conduct a special mission. Their objectives were: first, to study the effects of altitude on the human body, and second, to hunt for the yeti.

Ed led the search for the elusive yeti but he had no luck tracking one down. Disappointed but unsurprised, he tried another tack. Ed persuaded the monks at the monastery in Khumjung village, who had what they believed to be yeti scalps in their possession, to let him take a scalp to America for testing. The world watched and waited as scientists examined the skin.

Hopes of a breakthrough were dashed when the experts declared the scalps a fake. They had been molded from the skin of a serow—a type of antelope that lives in the Himalayas.

The mystery remained unsolved.

Sherpa belief says there are two types of yeti: the Metrey, which eats humans, and the Chutrey, which eats only smaller animals.

Metrey

Chutrey

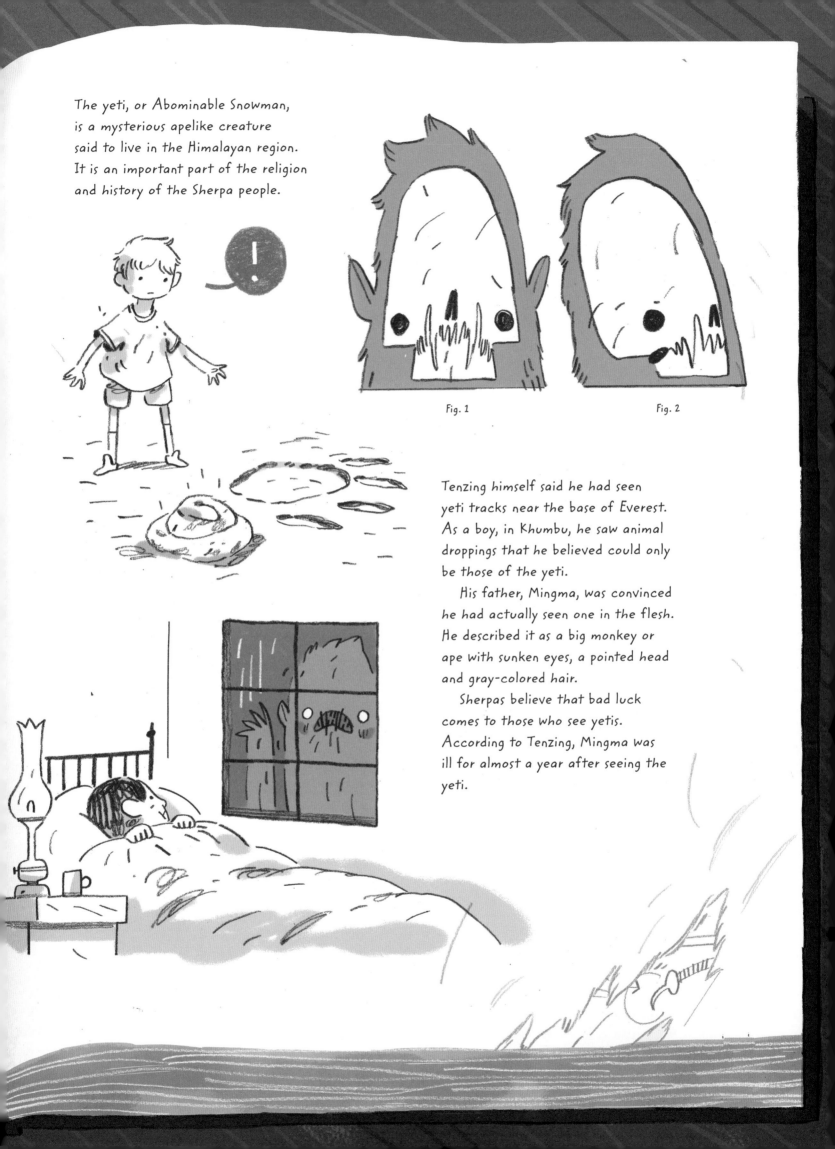

The yeti, or Abominable Snowman, is a mysterious apelike creature said to live in the Himalayan region. It is an important part of the religion and history of the Sherpa people.

Fig. 1

Fig. 2

Tenzing himself said he had seen yeti tracks near the base of Everest. As a boy, in Khumbu, he saw animal droppings that he believed could only be those of the yeti.

His father, Mingma, was convinced he had actually seen one in the flesh. He described it as a big monkey or ape with sunken eyes, a pointed head and gray-colored hair.

Sherpas believe that bad luck comes to those who see yetis. According to Tenzing, Mingma was ill for almost a year after seeing the yeti.

FROM THE OCEAN TO THE SKY

Over the next ten years, Edmund Hillary began to dedicate large amounts of time and energy to the welfare of the Sherpa people.

Ed and his wife, Louise, set up a charity called the Himalayan Trust to organize the work of building schools, water pipelines, bridges, and hospitals for other communities. In 1961, Ed opened the door of Khumjung's new Schoolhouse in the Clouds.

But in 1975 tragedy struck when Louise and 16-year-old Belinda were killed in a plane crash on their way to join Ed, who was building a large hospital in the Nepalese village of Phaplu. Heartbroken, Ed vowed to continue the projects that he and Louise had started. Phaplu Hospital was opened by Nepal's Prime Minister on May 1, 1976; it was the biggest project the Himalayan Trust had ever undertaken.

A year later, in 1977, Ed embarked on another great adventure. This time he was joined by his son, Peter. His plan was to pilot three jet boats up the Ganges. The Ganges is the longest river in India, flowing for more than 1,500 miles from its source in the Himalayas to the Bay of Bengal. It is regarded as sacred in the Hindu religion and is considered to be a crossing point between heaven and earth.

Heading to the source

Starting at the Bay of Bengal, Ed's aim was to get as close to the river's source as possible. It was something that he and Louise had often dreamed of doing.

After traveling for 1,300 miles upriver, Ed and his team reached the foothills of the Himalayas. Day after day, they forced their way up mighty rapids and through narrow gorges filled with rushing water. Although they could swim and wore life jackets, drowning in the wild water was an ever-present threat. Eventually their path was blocked by a vertical waterfall. Unable to go any farther, they got out of the water and began walking the final 100 miles.

They had decided they would complete their journey from ocean to sky by climbing a snowy peak called Akash Parbat. However, at 18,000 feet, Ed was struck down with cerebral edema, a potentially fatal condition where water builds up in the brain.

He was evacuated off the mountain by helicopter, lucky to be alive.

The diplomat

During his Ganges adventure, Ed developed a strong appreciation for the culture and religion of the Indian people. Little did he know that eight years later he would be back in India—but this time as New Zealand High Commissioner.

In February 1985, following a request from the New Zealand Prime Minister, Ed traveled to Delhi, where he began his first-ever nine-to-five job. As New Zealand's official representative on the ground, he was expected to help maintain and strengthen his country's relationship with India.

He was accompanied by June Mulgrew—the widow of one his Antarctica teammates and an old family friend. Ed had grown close to June after she had helped him with his charity work in Nepal. He was delighted to have her as his official companion.

Edmund Hillary and Neil Armstrong enjoy
frozen champagne at the North Pole.

TWO POLES

Ed's diplomatic career did not get in the way of his globetrotting, though.

Shortly after arriving in Delhi, Ed was invited to take a trip to the North Pole with another group of adventurers. Among them was the American astronaut Neil Armstrong—the first man to walk on the moon.

Unlike his previous adventures, this one was fairly tame. The team was delivered to the pole by a light aircraft, where they were handed a glass of frozen champagne. However, Ed was thrilled to become the first person to have stood at both the North and South Poles and the summit of Everest—often referred to as the Third Pole.

During his four years as High Commissioner, Ed established a good rapport with the Indian people. He and June bid farewell to India in 1989, and not long after returning to New Zealand they were married. Ed also became one of the first people to be awarded his country's highest honor: the Order of New Zealand. Nothing less would do for the man who had become a national hero and an international legend.

THE NEXT GENERATION

In 1990, Ed was sitting in his study at home when he received a phone call.

It was his son, Peter, calling up for a chat—from a satellite phone at the top of Everest! This was the moment that the Hillarys became the first father and son to have reached the summit of the world's tallest mountain.

Ed's son, Peter, makes a special call from the summit.

TENZING KEEPS CLIMBING

Like Edmund Hillary, Tenzing Norgay had climbed Everest as an ordinary man and descended as an international celebrity.

When he returned to his home in Darjeeling, he found he had become a symbol of hope and newfound confidence for the Indian people. In a country that had only recently gained independence from British rule, the man who had climbed from nothing to the top of the world represented a bright and promising new future.

Although he had achieved his ultimate climbing goal, mountaineering remained at the heart of Tenzing's life. In 1954, he became director of field training at the newly opened Himalayan Mountaineering Institute in Darjeeling. It would be his job to ensure future generations were taught the art of mountaineering.

A delighted Prime Minister Nehru, who was now a personal friend, told him, "Now you will make a thousand Tenzings." Tenzing remained director for 23 years. Later on, he became involved in organizing expeditions for wealthy and adventurous tourists.

In 1961, he married his third wife, Daku. Together, they had three sons: Norbu, Jamling, and Dhamey, and a daughter named Deki. Tenzing was determined that none of his children would suffer the hardships he had, telling them, "I climbed Everest so you wouldn't have to." Nevertheless, a Sherpa to the core, his son Jamling would go on to reach the summit in 1996.

When Ed became New Zealand High Commissioner to India in 1985, he had the opportunity to reestablish his friendship with Tenzing. By then, Tenzing was an aging and ill man. He had been sent to the hospital in Delhi after coming down with pneumonia. Tenzing's mastery of English had improved since the pair had scaled Everest, and Ed spent time by his bedside, talking with him about the past and the future. The bond they had forged 32 years previously became stronger than ever, and Tenzing drew comfort from his presence.

Hillary and Tenzing remember stories of their great triumph.

Tenzing died in 1986, aged 71. Just over ten years later, a statue of him was unveiled at the Himalayan Mountaineering Institute. Paying tribute to his friend and climbing partner, Ed told the gathered crowds:

"I have never regarded myself as much of a hero, but Tenzing, I believe, undoubtedly was. From humble beginnings he had achieved the summit of the world."

THE END OF AN ADVENTURE

Ed reached his 70s and had long ago called a halt to his high-altitude exploits.

Ed lived in Auckland with June where, despite his celebrity status, he led a modest and down-to-earth existence. He even allowed his contact information to remain in the public telephone directory. So, when a 14-year-old schoolboy called out of the blue to ask for help with his homework, Ed was happy to oblige.

Although he traveled less, Ed continued his charity work in Nepal. Thanks to his inspiration and drive, schools, hospitals, health clinics, bridges, and drinking-water systems were built, trees planted, Buddhist monasteries rebuilt and maintained, and scholarships awarded to Sherpas and Nepalese students.

Ed died in 2008, aged 88. In an honor usually reserved for the country's leaders, Sir Edmund Hillary's coffin lay in state in Holy Trinity Cathedral, Auckland. Members of the public lined up to pay their final respects to New Zealand's beloved son.

At his funeral, which was attended by 500 people from all over the world, New Zealand's then prime minister Helen Clark told the congregation: "Sir Ed described himself as a person of modest abilities. In reality, he was a colossus. He was our hero. He brought fame to our country. . . . Above all, we loved Sir Ed for what he represented: a determination to succeed against the odds, humility, and an innate sense of fair play."

"The greatest things I've done for the world aren't on mountains or in Antarctica, but have been doing projects with my friends the Sherpa people. These are the things I would like to be remembered for."